Starters & Sides

CRAB MEAT DIP

BAKED STUFFED CLAMS

OYSTER STEW

SUCCOTASH

STUFFED CHERRY TOMATOES

20	cherry tomatoes
1	cup Maryland backfin crabmeat
1	tablespoon mayonnaise
2	teaspoons parsley, finely chopped
2	teaspoons onion, finely chopped
1/2	teaspoon Worcestershire sauce
1/2	teaspoon seafood seasoning
	salt and pepper to taste
	parsley and paprika for garnish

Core tops of tomatoes. Combine remaining ingredients except garnish. Fill tomatoes. Sprinkle lightly with paprika and parsley. Serve hot or cold. To heat, bake in a preheated 375 degree oven for 10 minutes.

CRAB BALLS

1	pound Maryland crabmeat
1/2	cup breadcrumbs
1	egg
1/4	cup mayonnaise
1/2	teaspoon seafood seasoning ®Old Bay
1	teaspoon Worcestershire sauce
1	teaspoon dry mustard
1/2	teaspoon salt
1/4	teaspoon pepper

Mix together well all ingredients except crabmeat. Gently fold in the crabmeat. Form into 1/2 in. diameter balls and deep fry in oil heated to 365 degrees until brown and cooked through. Drain on paper towels and serve immediately. Makes about 12 balls.

CRAB-STUFFED MUSHROOMS

12	large or 24 medium sized mushrooms
5	tablespoons butter
2	tablespoons minced green onion
1	teaspoon lemon juice
1	cup flaked, cooked crab meat
1/2	cup soft bread crumbs
1	egg, lightly beaten
1/2	teaspoon dill weed
3/4	cup shredded Jack cheese
1/4	cup dry white wine
	lemon wedges

Wipe mushrooms with a damp cloth; remove the stems and finely chop them. Saute mushroom stems and onion in 2 tablespoons of the butter until onion is limp. Remove from heat and stir in lemon juice, crab, bread crumbs, egg, dill weed, and 1/4 cup of the cheese.

Melt remaining 3 tablespoons butter in a 9 by 13 inch baking pan. Turn mushroom caps in the butter to coat. Spoon about 2 tablespoons filling in each large cap (1 tablespoon in medium cap). Place mushrooms, filled side up in pan. Before baking, sprinkle mushrooms with remaining cheese and pour wine into pan. Bake in a 400 oven for 15 to 20 minutes. Serve hot with lemon wedges. Serves 6.

CRAB MEAT DIP

1	garlic clove
1/2	cup cream
1	8 ounce package cream cheese
1	cup crabmeat, flaked
2	teaspoons lemon juice
1-1/2	teaspoons Worcestershire sauce
	dash of pepper
	dash of salt

Rub bowl with garlic clove. Gradually add the cream to the cream cheese in the bowl blending until smooth. Add remaining ingredients and mix well. Yields 2 cups of dip.

OYSTERS ON THE HALF SHELL

6	fresh shucked oysters per serving
	lemon wedges
	hot pepper sauce
	ground black pepper
	buttered toast points

To shuck oysters, insert strong knife into hinge side of shell and twist to open. Loosen each oyster from the deeper half shell but let it remain in the shell. Discard other half. Serve on a bed of cracked ice around a small bowl of hot pepper sauce. Sprinkle with coarse ground black pepper and a squeeze of lemon. Serve with toast points.

bread crumbs and Parmesan cheese. Bake until heated through, about 10 minutes. Serves 2.

BAKED STUFFED CLAMS

12	medium-size cherrystone clams, well scrubbed
2	tablespoons water
	rock salt (optional)
2	tablespoons butter
2	shallots, finely chopped
2	cloves garlic, finely chopped
2	cups soft bread crumbs
1/4	cup finely chopped celery
2	tablespoons chopped parsley
1/2	teaspoon dry basil
1/2	teaspoon oregano
2	tablespoons freshly grated parmesan cheese
1	tablespoon olive oil
1	tablespoon dry white wine
	freshly ground black pepper
8	slices bacon, cut into thirds

Place the clams and water in a pan, cover and steam until clams open. Reserve the liquid, remove the clams from the shells and chop finely. Wash the shells and place on rock salt in shallow baking pan. Melt butter in a skillet and saute the shallots and garlic until just tender. Add the bread crumbs, celery, parsley, basil, oregano, cheese, oil, wine and pepper. Mix well. Stir in enough of reserved liquid to moisten crumbs but not make it soggy. Distribute the chopped clams among the shells, top with bread crumb mixture and a piece of the bacon. Bake in preheated 350 degree oven for 10 minutes and then broil until browned. Serves 4.

OYSTERS ROCKEFELLER

	rock salt
12	medium oysters in shell
1/4	cup butter
2	tablespoons onion, finely chopped
2	tablespoons celery, finely chopped
2	tablespoons snipped parsley
1/2	cup fresh spinach, chopped small
1/3	cup dry bread crumbs, divided
1/3	cup Parmesan cheese
	salt and pepper
	few drops of hot pepper sauce and
	worcestershire Sauce and anchovy Paste

Preheat oven to 450 degrees. Fill two 9" glass pie pans, or other oven-proof serving platters, with 1/2" rock salt. Prepare oysters for half shell as directed on page 3. Arrange filled shells on rock salt base. Melt butter in skillet and saute onion, celery and parsley until onion is tender. Mix in remaining ingredients, except one half of bread crumbs and Parmesan cheese. Spoon about 1 tablespoon spinach mixture onto oyster in each shell. Sprinkle with remaining

MARYLAND CRAB SOUP

2	tablespoons oil
1	carrot, diced
1	medium onion, diced
3	cups chicken broth
3	cups beef broth
3-4	cups diced potatoes
3-4	cups diced tomatoes (fresh or canned)
2	teaspoons seafood seasoning (®Old Bay)
1	pound Maryland crabmeat
2	tablespoons chopped parsley

Saute the carrot and onion in the oil in a stock pot. Cook until vegetables are softened. Add the broth, potatoes, tomatoes and seafood seasoning. Simmer just until the potatoes are tender, about 15 minutes. Add the crabmeat and parsley and heat through. Serves 4-5

CREAM OF CRAB SOUP

1	pound Maryland crabmeat (cartilage removed)
1/4	cup finely chopped onion
2	tablespoons butter
2	tablespoons flour
2	cups half-and-half
2	cups canned chicken broth
1	tablespoon dry sherry
	dash of hot pepper sauce
	salt and pepper to taste
	chopped parsley for garnish

Melt butter over low heat and saute the onion until translucent. Add the flour and cook for 4-5 minutes being careful not to brown the flour mixture. Stir in the broth and half-and-half, sherry and pepper sauce. Cook over low heat for about 10 minutes. Add the crabmeat and heat through. Adjust the seasoning. Serve immediately, garnish with parsley. Serves 4-6

CLAM CHOWDER

2	pounds clams (1 lb. shelled or canned clams)
3	oz. rindless bacon, diced
1	medium onion, finely diced
1	tablespoon flour
6	medium potatoes, peeled and cubed
4	cups milk
1	cup light cream
	chopped parsley (optional)

Saute bacon until fat is rendered. Remove bacon and set aside. Add onions to pan and cook until softened. Add the potatoes, salt, pepper, milk and reserved clam juice. Cover and boil twelve minutes or until potatoes are tender. Add the clams, cream, parsley and bacon and heat through. Do not boil. Serves 6.

TRADITIONAL MARYLAND OYSTER STEW

1	pint shucked Maryland oysters, with liquor
1	quart milk
1/4	cup butter
	salt, pepper and seafood seasoning to taste

In a large saucepan, cook oysters with liquor over low heat until edges of oysters just begin to curl. Add milk, butter, and seasonings. Heat slowly but do not boil.

CRAB AND PINEAPPLE SALAD

1	pineapple, cut in half lengthwise, remove center and chop
8	ounces lump Maryland crabmeat
1/4	cup walnuts, chopped
4	tablespoons parsley, chopped
1	apple, chopped
1	teaspoon lemon juice

DRESSING

1/4	cup rice vinegar
1/2	cup salad oil
3	tablespoons sugar
1/4	teaspoon salt
2	tablespoons onion, minced
1/4	cup pineapple, chopped
1	teaspoon celery salt

To make dressing, combine all ingredients in a blender and liquefy. Keep refrigerated.

Combine the crabmeat, pineapple, apple, lemon juice, walnuts and parsley, mix very gently. Line pineapple halves with lettuce and mound the salad in center. Just before serving, drizzle the dressing over the salad. Serves 2 generously.

MARYLAND-STYLE POTATO SALAD

3	cups cooked potatoes, diced
3	hard-boiled eggs, peeled and chopped
1/4	cup onion, diced
1/2	teaspoon dried oregano
1/4	teaspoon seafood seasoning
1/2	teaspoon dry mustard
1/3	cup mayonnaise
3	tablespoons sweet pickles, finely diced
	salt and pepper to taste

In a large bowl, mash together the potatoes and eggs. Add the remaining ingredients and mix lightly but thoroughly. Refrigerate for at least 3 hours before serving so flavors develop.

BOUILLABAISSE

A hearty fish stew, originated in Marseille, France and served throughout with a variety of different fish and shellfish. The original recipe called for 12 different types of fish.

1/2	cup olive oil
1	carrot, chopped
2	onions, chopped
2	leeks, chopped
2	cloves garlic, crushed

Heat olive oil in heavy kettle and saute vegetables until golden brown. Add:

2 - 3	pounds fish, boned and cut into 2" pieces
3	tomatoes, skinned and cut into wedges
4	potatoes, peeled and diced
1	bay leaf
3	cups fish stock, clam juice or water

Bring mixture to a boil and simmer 20 minutes. Add:

12	clams, oysters or mussels
12	raw shrimp, shelled and deveined
1	cup crab meat
	Salt and freshly ground pepper to taste
	juice of 1 lemon
1	cup dry white wine
8	slices french bread, toasted
2	sprigs chopped fresh parsley

Add all ingredients, except bread and parsley, and simmer 5 minutes. To serve, place the bread slices into 8 soup bowls and ladle the bouillabaisse over the bread. Sprinkle with chopped parsley. Serves 8.

CRAB SALAD

1	pound lump crab meat
2	hard-cooked eggs, chopped
1/2	cup celery, chopped
1	red pepper, seeded and diced
1/3	cup parsley, chopped
1/3	cup French dressing
	salt and pepper to taste
	spinach leaves

Mix all ingredients except spinach leaves. Season to taste. Serve on a bed of spinach leaves. Serves 6.

CHICKEN NOODLE SOUP

1	3 1/2 to 4 pound chicken, cut into serving pieces
2	quarts water
2	teaspoons salt
3	cups noodles
1	teaspoon peppercorns
1	small onion, chopped
1	carrot, sliced
1	bay leaf
2	tablespoons parsley, chopped
	salt and pepper

Simmer chicken in the water and salt until tender, about 45 minutes. Remove chicken and remove meat from bones. Add remaining ingredients, except noodles and chicken, and let boil again for 15 to 20 minutes. Add noodles and cook another 8-10 minutes. Add chicken, heat through and serve. Serves 8.

ROCKFISH SALAD

2	cups rockfish, poached, flaked and chilled
1/4	cup extra virgin olive oil
3	tablespoons lemon juice
1	teaspoon Dijon mustard
1	large clove garlic, minced
2	cups carrots, finely grated
1	tablespoon capers, drained
3	green onions, thinly sliced
1/2	cup fresh tarragon, or 1 tablespoon dried
3	plum tomatoes, sliced

Whisk together the olive oil, lemon juice, mustard, garlic and salt and pepper to taste. In a medium-sized bowl, add the fish and pour over it 1/2 of the vinaigrette. Stir lightly so all is moistened. Refrigerate for 30 minutes. Just before serving the salad, place the carrots in a large serving bowl. Add the capers, onions, and tarragon and toss. Pour over the remaining vinaigrette. Mound the carrot mixture on a large platter. Arrange the fish on top. Garnish with the sliced tomatoes. Serves 4.

Vegetables

SUCCOTASH

2	cups cooked, cubed ham
2-1/2	cups fresh lima beans
2-1/2	cups fresh corn
1	teaspoon salt
3/4	cup cream

Cook lima beans until almost tender. About 10 minutes before serving, add corn, diced ham and salt. Heat through, add hot cream. Serves 8.

FRIED ONION RINGS

1 1/2	cups flour
1 1/2	cups beer, flat or active
4	large, sweet yellow onions
4	cups shortening

Thoroughly mix together the flour and beer in a large bowl. Cover and allow the batter to sit at room temperature for at least 3 hours. Preheat oven to 225 degrees. Peel the onions and slice into 1/4 inch thick slices. Separate into rings. In the meantime, heat the shortening to 375 degrees (you will need to have the oil be at least 2 inches deep). Dip the rings into the batter and carefully place a few at a time in the hot oil. Fry until a golden brown. Drain on paper towels and place on a cookie sheet in preheated oven to keep warm until all rings are fried. Serve immediately. Serves 4-6

STUFFED BAKED EGGPLANT

2	firm eggplants
4	tablespoons shallots, finely chopped
1	tablespoon chopped parsley
1	stick butter
1	cup cooked shrimp
1	cup lump crab meat
	salt and pepper to taste
1	cup Parmesan cheese, finely grated
1/4	cup bread crumbs

Cut eggplants in half and place in the oven at 375 degrees in a pan with a cup of water in the bottom to steam the eggplant. Cook until tender, about thirty minutes. Carefully remove the pulp with a spoon so that you do not break the skin. Brown shallots and parsley in butter over low heat. Add shrimp, crab meat and the eggplant pulp. Season with salt and pepper. Stir together and cook for five minutes. Fill the shells. Sprinkle cheese and bread crumbs over the top of each eggplant. Bake at 350 degrees until tops are browned. Serves 4.

CORN FRITTERS

1	egg
2	tablespoons flour
2	teaspoons sugar
1/2	teaspoon baking powder
1	tablespoon milk
2	cups fresh corn kernels
3	green onions, finely sliced
3	egg whites
3	tablespoons butter
	salt and pepper to taste

Whisk together the egg, flour, sugar, baking powder, salt and pepper. Stir in the milk, corn, and onion. In a separate bowl, beat the 3 egg whites until stiff peaks form. Fold egg whites into corn mixture. In a non-stick skillet, heat the butter until foamy. Spoon large spoonfuls of batter into pan. (4 at a time in a 12 in. skillet) Cook over medium heat about 3 minutes per side. Makes 12 fritters.

FRIED GREEN TOMATOES

6	green tomatoes
4	tablespoons butter
2/3	cup flour
1	teaspoon ©Old Bay Seasoning
	salt and pepper to taste
1/2	cup milk
2	tablespoons brown sugar

Cut tomatoes into 1/2 inch slices. Mix together the flour, salt and pepper and ©Old Bay seasoning. In a frying pan, melt 3 tablespoons of the butter. Dredge the slices of tomato in the flour mixture and fry the floured tomatoes until browned on both sides. After all the tomatoes are fried, add the remaining butter, milk and 1 tablespoon of the remaining flour mixture to the pan drippings. Cook and stir until sauce is thickened. Pour over tomatoes and top with the brown sugar.

Main Course

STEAMED BLUE CRABS

BAKED STUFFED ROCKFISH

CRAB CAKES

MARYLAND FRIED CHICKEN

Ah, the blue crab. Anyone who has enjoyed a summertime feast of a pile of spicy steamed crabs will understand why the crab's zoological name, Callinectes sapidus, means beautiful swimmer. To truly enjoy your crab feast, follow these easy steps and soon you'll be considered a local.

- Dump the cooked crabs on a table covered with newspaper.
- Flip the crab over, lift off the apron
- Flip off the top shell, you will see "all this stuff hanging out", pull it out and throw them on the paper
- The yellow stuff in the middle is the "mustard". Actually it's fat and quite delicious. Eat it!
- Break the body in half, leaving the legs and claws on.
- Squish down the backfin and twist it around. You'll get a succulent piece of crab meat.

- Pull the swimming legs and claws off the body, one by one. There will be a little piece of meat at the end of each. Suck it and save the claw portion.
- With a knife split each half of the crab horizontally. This exposes chambers where the delicious crabmeat is waiting for your enjoyment.
- Take a big claw and break it apart at the joint. Now with a mallet drive a paring knife through the claw and carefully pull out a whole piece of meat.
  Repeat the above until you've had your fill.

STEAMED BLUE CRABS

2	12- ounce cans beer, allowed to go flat
2	cups white vinegar
1/2	cup Old Bay® seasoning
1/2	cup rock salt
18-24	large live male blue crabs (jimmies)

Mix first 4 ingredients together. In a large steamer pot with a tight-fitting lid, put 1/2 of the crabs on a rack. Cover with 1/2 of the seasoning mixture. Add rest of crabs and remaining seasoning. Steam, covered, until crabs turn bright red in color, about 20-30 minutes. Serves 4 depending on size of crabs.

THE CRAB FEAST

At a crab feast, many traditionalists enjoy nothing else but the crab. Others might include some of the following:

- Bowls of vinegar and melted butter.
- Platters of sliced tomatoes.
- Mounds of Silver Queen sweet corn on the cob.
- Assorted salads such as coleslaw, potato, greens with fresh vegetables.
- Desserts could be watermelon, strawberry shortcake, peach cobbler, or ice cream.

BAKED SEAFOOD SALAD

1/2	cup green pepper, chopped
1/4	cup onion, minced
1	cup celery, chopped
1	cup crab meat, cooked or canned
1	cup shrimp, cooked or canned
1	cup mayonnaise
1/2	teaspoon salt
1	teaspoon Worcestershire sauce
2	cups corn flakes, crushed, or l cup fine dry bread crumbs
	dash of paprika
2	tablespoons butter or margarine
	lemon slices

Combine green pepper, onion, celery, fish, mayonnaise, salt and Worcestershire. Mix lightly. Place mixture into individual shells or shallow baking dish. Sprinkle with crushed corn flakes or crumbs and paprika. Dot with butter. Bake at 350 degrees about 30 minutes. Serve with slices of lemon. Serves 6.

CRAB MEAT IMPERIAL

1	green pepper, finely diced
2	pimientos, finely diced
1	tablespoon Dijon mustard
1	teaspoon salt
1/2	teaspoon white pepper
2	whole eggs
1	cup mayonnaise
3	pounds lump crab meat

Mix pepper and pimientos. Add mustard, salt, white pepper, eggs and mayonnaise. Mix well. Add crab meat, mixing gently so that lumps are not broken. Divide mixture into 6 crab shells or casseroles, heaping it in lightly. Top with a coating of mayonnaise and sprinkle with paprika. Bake at 350 degrees for 15 minutes. Serve hot or cold. Serves 6.

CRAB NEWBURG

4	tablespoons butter
2	cups cooked crab meat
1/4	cup Madeira or dry sherry
1/2	teaspoon paprika
1/8	teaspoon ground nutmeg
3	egg yolks
1	cup cream

In a double boiler, melt the butter. Add the crab meat and cook about 2 minutes. Add the Madeira and spices. Beat together the egg yolks and cream and add to crab mixture. Cook and stir constantly until thickened. Do not boil.

Remove from heat and serve over hot buttered toast points. Serves 4.

FRIED FANTAIL SHRIMP IN BEER BATTER

1	cup sifted flour
1/2	teaspoon sugar
1/2	teaspoon salt
1	teaspoon baking powder
1	egg, beaten
1	cup beer
	dash of pepper
	dash of nutmeg
2	pounds fresh shrimp
	cooking oil

Stir all ingredients, except shrimp, into a batter. Peel shell from shrimp, leaving the last section and tail intact. Cut almost through shrimp at the center back without cutting ends. Dry shrimp and dip into beer batter. Fry in deep, hot fat until golden brown. Drain and serve at once. Serves 4.

FRIED CLAMS

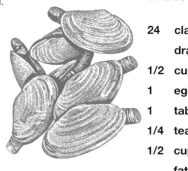

24	clams, shucked and drained
1/2	cup milk
1	egg, separated
1	tablespoon butter
1/4	teaspoon salt
1/2	cup flour
	fat for deep frying

Beat the egg yolk with 1/4 cup milk. Stir in the butter, salt and flour and beat until smooth. Gradually beat in remaining milk. Beat the egg white until stiff. Fold into batter. Dip each clam into the batter and fry in hot fat (375 degrees). Serves 3-4.

DEVILED CRAB

1	pound fresh crab meat, (or thawed)
2	tablespoons butter or margarine
1	cup milk
2	tablespoons flour
1	teaspoon dry mustard
	dash cayenne pepper or hot pepper sauce
1	tablespoon parsley, minced
1	teaspoon onion, minced
1	teaspoon Worcestershire sauce
1/2	cup sharp Cheddar cheese, grated

Saute crab meat several minutes in butter. Add milk and seasonings, with more salt, if necessary. Fill individual shells or casseroles with the mixture and top with cheese. Bake until lightly browned on top, about 20 minutes, at 375 degrees. Serves 4.

ESCALLOPED OYSTERS

1	pint (2 cups) oysters with liquor
2	cups coarsely crushed saltine crackers
1/4	cup butter
1/4	teaspoon salt
1/4	teaspoon pepper
1/2	cup light cream

Cut oysters into 3-4 pieces each with kitchen shears. Combine them with their liquor. Butter a shallow baking dish. Arrange a layer of cracker crumbs. Then put on layer of oysters, salt, pepper and dots of butter. Repeat layer of crackers and oysters. Top with remaining cracker crumbs. Pour the cream over all. Bake in a preheated 350 degree oven for 30 minutes. Serves 4.

GRILLED MARYLAND BLUEFISH

2	pounds bluefish fillets (skinned)
1 1/2	cups bottled Italian salad dressing
3	lemons, cut in wedges

Place fillets in a baking dish. Pour dressing over fish, cover and refrigerate for 2 hours. Place fillets on a hot, oiled grill. Baste frequently with dressing and cook about 8 minutes. Turn and baste again. Test with a fork to see if fish flakes (indication it is done).

SCAMPI

6	tablespoons butter
1/4	cup olive oil
2	tablespoons parsley, minced
2	garlic cloves, minced
1/2	teaspoon salt
2	tablespoons lemon juice
1	pound large shrimp

Preheat oven to 450 degrees. Melt the butter and add the olive oil, parsley, garlic, salt and lemon juice. Mix well. Shell and devein the shrimp, leaving the tails attached. Split down the inside lengthwise, being careful not to cut through the shrimp. Spread open to simulate butterflies. Place in a shallow baking pan, tail end up. Pour sauce over all. Bake for 5 minutes. Place under broiler for 5 minutes longer to brown. Serves 4.

FETTUCCINE WITH SHRIMP & SCALLOPS

1	pound fettuccine pasta
3/4	pound medium shrimp, peeled and deveined
1/2	pound medium scallops
2	ounces fresh basil
3	cloves garlic, chopped
1/4	cup olive oil
2	cups fish stock or clam juice
	parsley
	pine nuts

Saute garlic in 1/4 cup olive oil for 1 minute. Add shrimp and scallops and cook for 4 minutes. Add basil, parsley and 2 cups fish stock or clam juice. Simmer for 10 minutes. Serve over cooked fettuccine. Top with pine nuts. Serves 4.

The gastronomic delicacy known as the "Soft-shell Crab" has a most interesting life history. In the brackish waters in the Chesapeake Bay live the blue crabs, who throughout their short life span of 2-4 years, shed their hard outer shell as many as 20 times. Watermen (those who dredge the waters for these peelers, busters, snots and softs- local slang for these dennisens of the Chesapeake) gather up these gems in an effort to satisfy the tastes of the gourmet diner around the globe. Locally, this seafood delight that has made the Chesapeake Bay famous is common everyday fare. The 'peelers' are harvested from mid-May throughout the summer and into early fall. The Chesapeake Bay area accounts for 90 percent of the United States soft-shell crab production.

DEEP-FRIED CHESAPEAKE BAY SOFT-SHELLED CRABS

1	cup flour
1	teaspoon salt
1/2	teaspoon baking powder
1/2	teaspoon paprika
1	12 ounce can beer, allowed to go flat
6	large soft-shell crabs, cleaned
	oil for frying

Mix dry ingredients together in bowl. Stir in the beer, mix until well blended. Let stand at room temperature for 1 hour. Heat oil in deep fat fryer to 375 degrees. Dust the prepared crabs with flour, then coat with the batter. Slip carefully into the hot fat. Fry only 1 or 2 at a time so oil does not cool off. Fry until golden brown, drain on paper towels and serve immediately. Serves 3.

CRAB CAKES

1	pound crab meat, picked over
1/4	cup onion diced
1/4	cup red bell pepper, diced
3	cups fresh bread crumbs
1/2	cup mayonnaise
1/4	cup cream cheese, softened
1	tablespoon dijon mustard
1	egg, slightly beaten
1/2	teaspoon dried leaf tarragon
1/8	teaspoon cayenne pepper
1/8	teaspoon salt
2	tablespoons vegetable oil
	lemon wedges or slices to serve

Drain crab meat well. Combine crab meat, onion, bell pepper and 1/2 cup of the bread crumbs in a medium size bowl. Beat mayonnaise, cream cheese, mustard, egg, tarragon, cayenne and salt together in a separate bowl. Stir mayonnaise mixture into crab meat mixture. Cover and refrigerate 30 minutes. Place remaining crumbs into a shallow bowl. Using an oval soup spoon, drop spoonfuls of mixture onto crumbs and form into patties, coating each side with crumbs. Heat oil in a skillet over medium heat. Carefully add crab cakes. Cook until golden brown, turning once. If oil browns, wipe out skillet and add fresh oil. Serve with lemon. Makes 24 appetizer size crab cakes or 6 entree size cakes.

STEAMED CLAMS

1/4	cup butter
6	chopped shallots
1	clove garlic
1/4	cup dry white wine
1	bay leaf
36-48	scrubbed steamer clams

Saute the shallots and garlic in the butter until softened. Add the wine and bay leaf. Carefully add the clams and cook covered until clams open.

Pour the clams, shells and all into heated bowls and serve garnished with chopped parsley. A crusty country loaf to accompany this is great for soaking up the broth. Serves 4-6.

CRAB MEAT QUICHE

	pastry for a single crust 9" pie
1	tablespoon butter
1	tablespoon celery, chopped
1	tablespoon onions, chopped
1-1/2	cups crab meat, picked over well to remove shell or cartilage
2	tablespoons parsley, chopped
2	tablespoons sherry
4	eggs, lightly beaten
1	cup milk
1	cup cream
1/4	teaspoon nutmeg, grated
1/2	teaspoon salt
1/4	teaspoon white pepper

Preheat oven to 375 degrees. Line a 9" pie pan with pastry and line pastry with foil. Add dried beans to weight the bottom down and bake 30 minutes. Remove the foil and beans. Melt butter in a skillet and saute the celery and onions until wilted. Add the crab meat and cook over high heat until any liquid has evaporated. Stir in the parsley and sherry. Sprinkle the inside of the baked pastry shell with the crab meat mixture. Combine eggs, milk, cream, nutmeg, salt and pepper and pour over the crab mixture in the pie. Bake 40 minutes, or until knife inserted comes out clean. Cut into wedges and serve immediately. Serves 6.

SCALLOPS AND SPINACH NOODLES

2	carrots, peeled and julienned
1	green pepper, julienned
6	green onions, jullienned
1/2	cup butter
3/4	cup dry white wine
1	pound scallops, cut into slices
1	cup whipping cream
1/2	pound spinach noodles
	grated nutmeg
	salt and pepper to taste

Melt 2 tablespoons of the butter in a skillet. Add the vegetables and saute quickly. Remove the vegetables and set aside. Add wine and bring to a boil. Add the scallops and cook about 3 minutes. Remove scallops from pan and set aside. Add cream to pan liquid and bring to a boil. On low heat slowly add remaining butter until butter melts. Meanwhile, cook noodles, drain and rinse. Add to the cream mixture. add scallops and vegetables. Mix gently. Season to taste with salt, pepper and grated nutmeg. Serves 4.

BAKED STUFFED ROCKFISH

1 1/2	pounds rockfish filets (Striped Bass)
1/2	recipe Crab Imperial (page 14)
	salt and pepper to taste

Place 1/2 of filets of Rockfish in a greased baking dish. Season with salt and pepper. Divide the crab imperial mixture evenly over the filets. Cover with remaining half of filets. Brush with melted butter, sprinkle with paprika and bake in a 350 degree preheated oven for approximately 25-30 minutes depending on thickness of filets. Serves 4

JUMBO STEAMED SHRIMP

1/2	cup vinegar
1	tablespoon seafood seasoning (®Old Bay)
1	teaspoon salt
3/4	cup water
1 1/2	pounds jumbo shrimp

In a saucepan combine the vinegar, seasoning, salt and water. Bring to a boil. Add shrimp. Stir gently to coat the shrimp with the liquid. Cover and steam for 5-8 minutes or until shrimp are cooked. Drain and serve. Serves 4-5

STEAMED MUSSELS

1/2	cup dry white wine
1	bay leaf
1	teaspoon finely chopped fresh thyme (or 1/2 teas. dried thyme)
1/2	onion, finely chopped
1	clove garlic, chopped
	salt and pepper to taste
2	tablespoons chopped parsley
3-4	pounds mussels, well scrubbed and beards removed

Combine first 6 ingredients in large kettle or skillet. Add the mussels and cover. Cook about 7 minutes or until mussels open. Serve immediately with broth and sprinkle with the chopped parsley. Serves 4

JAMBALAYA

2	tablespoons butter
1	medium green pepper, chopped
1/2	cup celery, chopped
1/2	cup onion, chopped
1/2	cup parsley, chopped
1	16 ounce can tomatoes, diced
2	cups chicken broth (canned)
1/2	teaspoon salt
1/8	teaspoon pepper
1	teaspoon chili powder
3	bay leaves
2	cups cooked rice
2	cups (1 pint) Maryland oysters, drained
1/2	pound white fish, cubed
1	pound Maryland crabmeat

Saute the green pepper, celery and onion in the butter for 5 minutes in a large saucepan. Add the parsley, tomatoes, water, stock and seasonings and simmer over medium heat for 30-40 minutes. Add the rice, oysters and fish and simmer for 10 minutes. Add the crabmeat and simmer 5 more minutes. Serves 6

SHAD ROE

10	strips bacon
2	medium onions
4	pairs small shad roe
4	tablespoons lemon juice
5	tablespoons flour
1/2	teaspoon each salt and lemon pepper
1/4	teaspoon fine herbs
	lemon slices and parsley for garnish

In skillet, fry bacon and onions until cooked. In the meantime, combine flour and spices in a shallow plate. Rinse off the shad roe and sprinkle with lemon juice. Dredge shad roe in flour mixture and place in skillet with bacon and onions. Cover and cook over medium heat for 5 minutes. Sprinkle with parsley and serve with lemon slices. Serves 4

CHICKEN FRICASSEE WITH DUMPLINGS

1	4-6 pound chicken, cut into serving pieces
5	cups boiling water
4	stalks celery
1	medium onion, chopped
1/4	cup parsley, chopped
2	teaspoons salt
1	teaspoon sugar
1/2	cup flour
1/4	teaspoon pepper
1	cup light cream or half and half
2	cups fresh or frozen peas
	parsley dumplings (recipe follows)

Simmer chicken in large covered kettle with the next 6 ingredients until chicken is tender, about 45 minutes. Remove chicken and keep hot. Reserve the stock and add water or chicken broth to make 5 cups. Mix together in small jar the flour, pepper and cream. Shake until well blended. Heat the 5 cups cooking liquid to boiling. Add the flour mixture, stirring until thickened. Season to taste. In the meantime, make the dumpling mixture. Drop by spoonfuls onto the gently boiling liquid. Cover kettle tightly and cook 15-20 minutes without lifting lid. To serve, spoon the dumplings and sauce over chicken on serving plate. Serves 6-8.

PARSLEY DUMPLINGS

2	cups flour
4	teaspoons baking powder
1	teaspoon salt
1/4	cup melted shortening (butter preferred)
1-1/4	cups milk
1/2	cup parsley, finely chopped

Mix together the dry ingredients. Combine the cooled melted shortening with the milk and parsley and add all at once to the dry ingredients. Stir just until dry ingredients are moistened.

SPIT-BARBECUED CHICKEN

1	3 pound whole chicken
1/4	cup cooking oil
2	teaspoons salt
1	recipe maple syrup-apple cider glaze

Arrange fire for spit barbecuing by placing briquets in a heaping layer to one side of the fire box, leaving room to place a drip pan directly beneath the meat. Rub chicken inside and out with cooking oil. Put 2 teaspoons salt in the cavity. When coals are hot, knock off any gray ash. Place chicken on skewer so that it is evenly balanced. Use heavy twine to tie wings to the body and legs to each other securely. Place the drip pan under the meat and start the motor. Brush chicken with more cooking oil. Insert meat thermometer in the thickest part of the thigh at an angle so that it will not hit the briquets of the hood as it rotates. Baste chicken often with more oil. Cook 1 to 1-1/2 hours; thermometer should read 190 degrees when done. During last 15 minutes, baste chickens with glaze. Remove from spit; cut and remove twine before serving. Serve with additional glaze. Serves 4.

MAPLE SYRUP-APPLE CIDER GLAZE

1	cup maple syrup
1/2	cup apple cider
1	tablespoon butter
1	teaspoon salt

Combine ingredients in a saucepan and bring to a boil. Reduce heat to low. Baste chicken during last 15 minutes of cooking. Makes enough for 3 chickens; or for 1 chicken with sauce remaining to serve to the table.

ROAST TURKEY CHESAPEAKE STYLE

1	14-16 pound fresh turkey
	salt and pepper to taste

OYSTER STUFFING

3	stalks celery, chopped
1	medium onion, chopped
3/4	cup butter
1/2	teaspoon salt
1/2	teaspoon pepper
1/4	teaspoon mace
1/2	teaspoon tarragon
1	teaspoon poultry seasoning
1	teaspoon lemon juice
3	cups shucked Maryland oysters with liquor
12	slices day-old bread, left out to dry and cubed

Saute the celery and onions in the butter until tender. Add the seasonings. Add the oysters and simmer until the edges of the oysters begin to curl. Remove from heat and gently mix in the bread cubes. Add water or clam juice to make sure the stuffing is moist. Season turkey on inside and outside with salt and pepper, fill turkey cavity with the stuffing and cook the turkey according to directions. (about 20 minutes per pound in a 325 degree oven). Do not cover and roast breast side up. Baste with the pan drippings every 20 minutes. Tent the turkey with foil if it is browning too quickly.

CRAB-STUFFED CHICKEN BREAST

2	skinless, boneless, half chicken breasts
1/2	cup lump crab meat
1	teaspoon ©Old Bay seasoning
3/4	cup flour
2	eggs, lightly beaten
1/4	cup onion, diced
1/4	cup green pepper, diced
1	tablespoon dijon mustard
1/4	cup mayonnaise
1	cup dry bread crumbs
	vegetable oil for frying

Gently season the crab meat with the ©Old Bay seasoning and then add the onion, green pepper, mustard and mayonnaise.Between 2 sheets of plastic wrap, gently pound the chicken breasts into 6-7 inch rounds. (do not make any holes in the meat) Remove the wrap and place 1/2 of the crab mixture in center of flattened chicken breast. Roll up, folding in sides so filling is completely enclosed. Secure with toothpicks if necessary. Dip the chicken rolls into the beaten egg, then in the flour. Coat with the bread crumbs and fry in a deep fryer with vegetable oil preheated to 375 degrees. Cook about 5 minutes until golden brown. Drain on paper towels. Remove toothpicks (if used) before serving. Serves 2

MARYLAND FRIED CHICKEN WITH CREAM GRAVY

1	3 to 4 pound frying chicken, cut into 8 pieces
1	cup all-purpose flour for dredging
1	teaspoon poultry seasoning
	vegetable oil for frying
1	tablespoon butter
2	tablespoon flour
1	cups milk
1	cup half-and-half
1	cup canned chicken broth

Rinse the chicken and pat it dry. Sprinkle with salt and pepper to suit your taste. Mix together the flour, and poultry seasoning. Dredge the chicken in flour mixture and set aside to rest 15 minutes. Meanwhile put enough vegetable oil in a large heavy skillet to a depth of about 1/2 inch. Heat to about 365 degrees. Put the legs and thighs in hot oil first, cover and fry about 5 minutes. Turn the pieces and add the remaining chicken pieces. Cover and cook another 5 minutes. Uncover and turn the chicken. Cook uncovered, turning occasionally until chicken is brown, crisp and cooked through (about 25 minutes total cooking time).

Remove chicken to platter and keep warm. Pour all but 2 tablespoons of fat from pan. Add the butter and 2 tablespoons flour to pan and cook for 1 minute while stirring over medium heat. Add the half-and-half, milk and broth to pan and stir well. Cook over low heat until thickened, about 5 minutes. Taste for seasoning and adjust. Serve over the chicken or separately. Serves 4-6

Breads & Desserts

CORNBREAD

PEACH PIE

BREAD PUDDING

FUDGE BROWNIES

PAN ROLLS

Breads

CORNBREAD

1-1/2   cups yellow cornmeal
1   cup all-purpose flour, sifted
1   tablespoon baking powder
1- 1/4 teaspoons salt
3/4   cup (l and 1/2 sticks) unsalted butter,
        melted and cooled
2   large eggs, lightly beaten
1-1/2   cups milk

Preheat oven to 375 degrees. Butter a 9 inch square pan. In a mixing bowl, sift together the cornmeal, flour, baking powder and salt. Add the butter, eggs and milk and stir until just combined. Pour into pan and bake about 40 minutes; or divide mix into corn stick mold pan and bake 20 minutes. Or double the recipe, pour into a greased heavy cast iron skillet that has been preheated. Bake for 25 to 30 minutes. Yields 6-9 servings.

YEASTED ROSEMARY BREAD WITH RAISINS

5-7   cups flour
2   teaspoons salt
2-3   tablespoons sugar
2   teaspoons instant yeast
2   tablespoons rosemary, chopped
1/4-1/2 cup olive oil
2 - 2-1/2 cups warm water, approximately
1/2   cup raisins

Combine about 4 cups flour with remainder of dry ingredients, including instant yeast. Add olive oil and enough warm water to make a sticky dough. Use more flour to bring mass together into a smooth, slightly sticky, elastic dough. Knead well. Add raisins. Allow to double. Shape into loaf. Allow to double again. Preheat oven to 375 degrees. Bake about 45 minutes, then cool I hour before cutting.

ORANGE ROLLS

4	tablespoons butter or margarine
1/4	cup sugar
1	cup milk, scalded and cooled to lukewarm
1	package yeast, active dry or compressed
1/4	cup warm water (lukewarm for compressed yeast)
1	egg, slightly beaten
4	cups all-purpose flour, sifted softened butter and sugar

ORANGE FILLING:

3	tablespoons butter or margarine, softened
1	tablespoon grated orange peel
2	tablespoons orange juice
1-1/2	cups confectioners sugar

Place the butter, salt and sugar in a large bowl. Add the milk, stirring to dissolve the sugar and salt and to melt butter. Soften the yeast in the warm water and add it and the beaten egg to the milk mixture. Stir in 3-1/2 cups of flour, 1 cup at a time, beating vigorously to blend. Scrape dough from the sides of the bowl. Place on floured board and knead until smooth. (Do not use more than 1/4 to 1/2 cup flour on the board). Return to bowl (greased lightly). Cover with towel and let rise in draft free warm area until doubled (about 1-1/2 hours).

While dough is rising, prepare the filling. With mixer, blend the softened butter, sugar, orange peel and juice until smooth. If necessary add more juice or sugar until mixture is spreadable.

Turn out risen dough onto floured board and roll out into a 12" X 15" rectangle. Spread with orange filling. Roll up like a jelly roll and cut into 1 1/2" slices. Place each slice in a well greased muffin tin. Sprinkle with sugar. Cover and let rise until doubled. Bake in preheated oven at 375° for 12 - 15 minutes. When done, turn out immediately by inverting pan. Makes 8 large or 12 medium rolls.

STICKY BUNS

Make a dough as in recipe for Orange Rolls. When ready to make into rolls after last rising, roll out dough into a 12" X 15" rectangle and spread with 3 tablespoons softened butter, sprinkle with 1 teaspoon cinnamon and 1/4 cup brown sugar. Roll as you would a jelly roll. Slice into 1-1/2 inch slices and place cut side down into prepared pan. Let rise until doubled (about 1 hour). Bake in preheated oven at 350° for 30 - 40 minutes. Remove from oven, let stand 1 minute. Invert to remove rolls and to let the caramel cover the rolls.

While dough is rising, prepare the baking dish. Heat 1 cup brown sugar and 1/2 cup butter in saucepan until thoroughly blended. Stir constantly until sugar is dissolved. Remove from heat and add 1/4 cup dark corn syrup. Pour into a 9" X 13" baking dish. sprinkle with 1 cup pecans. Raisins may also be added.

Cover and let rise in warm place about 30 minutes or until double. Heat oven to 400 degrees. Bake 12 to 18 minutes or until golden brown. Makes 48 rolls.

Cloverleaf Rolls: Grease bottoms and sides of 24 medium muffin cups, 2-1/2x1-1/4 inches, with shortening. After punching down dough, cut dough in half; cut each half into 36 pieces. Shape into balls. Place 3 balls in each muffin cup. Brush with margarine. Cover and let rise in warm place about 30 minutes or until double. Bake as directed for pan rolls above. Makes 24 rolls.

PAN ROLLS

3-1/2 - 3-3/4 cups all-purpose flour

1/4	cup sugar
1/4	cup shortening
1	teaspoon salt
1	package regular or fast-acting active dry yeast
1/2	cup very warm water (120 to 130 degrees)
1/2	cup very warm milk (120 to 130 degrees)
1	large egg margarine or butter, melted

Mix 2 cups of the flour, the sugar, shortening, salt and yeast in medium bowl. Add warm water, warm milk and egg. Beat with electric mixer on low speed 1 minute, scraping bowl frequently. Beat on medium speed 1 minute, scraping bowl frequently. Stir in enough remaining flour to make dough easy to handle. Turn dough onto lightly floured surface. Knead about 5 minutes or until smooth and elastic. Place in greased bowl and turn greased side up. Cover and let rise in warm place about 1 hour or until double. Dough is ready if indentation remains when touched.

Grease bottoms and sides of 2 round pans, 9x1-1/2 inches, with shortening. Punch dough down. Cut dough in half; cut each half into 24 pieces. Shape into balls. Place close together in pans. Brush with margarine.

SPOON BREAD

2-1/2	cups milk
2	teaspoons sugar
1	teaspoon salt
1	cup yellow corn meal
3	eggs, separated
3	tablespoons butter

Place milk in top of double boiler and heat to boiling point. Add salt, sugar and corn meal, stirring constantly to prevent lumps. Cook 4 minutes and pour slowly over beaten yolks. Add butter and beat until it is melted. Fold in stiffly beaten whites and pour in greased deep casserole or souffle dish. Bake at 400 degrees for 45 minutes. Serves 8.

Desserts

PEACH PIE

	pastry for two crust pie
1/3	cup sugar
1/3	cup all-purpose flour
1/4	teaspoon ground nutmeg
6	cups (about 6 to 8 medium) peaches, uniformly sliced
1	teaspoon lemon juice
1	tablespoon margarine or butter

Heat oven to 400 degrees. Prepare pastry. Mix sugar, flour and cinnamon in large bowl. Stir in peaches and lemon juice. Turn into pastry-lined pie plate. Dot with margarine. Cover with top pastry and cut slits in it; seal and flute edges. Cover edge with a 2 to 3 inch strip of aluminum foil to prevent excessive browning. Remove foil during last 15 minutes of baking. Bake about 45 minutes or until crust is brown and juice begins to bubble through slits in crust. Cool in pie plate on wire rack. Serve warm or cool. Yields 8 servings.

SUGAR COOKIES

1	cup butter
1	cup confectioners sugar
1	cup granulated sugar
2	eggs
1	cup oil
2	teaspoons vanilla
1	teaspoon baking soda
1	teaspoon cream of tartar
1/2	teaspoon salt
5	cups flour
	granulated sugar for dipping

In medium bowl, cream butter with confectioners sugar and granulated sugar. Beat in eggs until smooth. Slowly stir in oil, vanilla, baking soda, cream of tartar, salt and flour. Chill for easy handling. Shape into walnut-size balls. Dip in sugar. Place on baking sheet and press down. Bake in preheated oven at 350 degrees for 10 -12 minutes. Makes about 4 dozen cookies.

BLUEBERRY COFFEE CAKE

1 1/2	cups flour
3/4	cup sugar
2 1/2	teaspoons baking powder
1	teaspoon salt
1/2	cup vegetable oil
3/4	cup milk
1	egg
1 1/2	cups blueberries

Blend together the dry ingredients. Add the oil and milk and mix thoroughly. Gently fold in 1 cup of the blueberries. Spread into a greased 8 or 9 in. square pan. Sprinkle the topping over this and top with the remaining blueberries. Bake in a preheated 375° oven for 25-30 minutes. Do not overbake. Serves 6-8.

TOPPING

1/3 cup flour; 1/2 cup brown sugar, firmly packed; 1/2 teaspoon cinnamon; 1/4 cup cold butter.
Cut butter into dry ingredients. Mixture will be crumbly.

CARAMEL NUT RING

1/2	cup butter
1/2	cup chopped pecans
1	cup brown sugar, firmly packed
2	tablespoons water
2	(8 ounce) cans crescent dinner rolls

Melt butter in small saucepan. Use 2 tablespoons to coat bottom and sides of 12-cup bundt pan. Sprinkle pan with 3 tablespoons of chopped pecans. Add remaining nuts, brown sugar, and water to remaining butter. Heat to a boil, stirring occasionally. Remove dinner rolls from can but do not unroll. Cut each can of rolls into 16 slices, cut side up, in bottom of pan, overlapping slices. Spread half the caramel nut sauce over slices. Repeat next layer with second can of rolls and top with remaining caramel sauce. Bake at 350 degrees for 25-30 minutes or until golden brown. Cool 3 minutes. Turn onto serving platter and slice. Freezes well. Serves 8 to 10.

CHOCOLATE CRAZY CAKE

2	cups sugar
2	cups flour
1	cup butter or margarine, softened
1/4	cup cocoa
1	cup hot water
2	eggs, beaten
1	teaspoon baking soda
1	teaspoon vanilla
1/2	cup buttermilk

Sift sugar and flour together. Combine butter and cocoa with hot water, mixing well. Pour over sugar and flour mixture. Add eggs, soda, vanilla and buttermilk. Stir only a few times until well blended. Put into a greased and floured 9 x 13 inch cake pan. Bake at 350 degrees for about 30 to 35 minutes. While cake is baking, prepare icing.

ICING

Mix together 2 cups confectioners sugar, 1/4 cup milk and 1/2 teaspoon vanilla. If too thin, add a little more confectioners sugar. After cake cools about 15 minutes, spread icing over cake while still warm.

APPLE PIE

	pastry for 2 crust pie
6	cups tart apples like Granny Smith, peeled and sliced
2/3	cup sugar
3	tablespoons flour
1	teaspoon lemon juice
1-2	teaspoons cinnamon
1/2	teaspoon nutmeg
2	tablespoons butter

Line a deep 9 inch pie pan with pastry. In a large bowl, mix together the sliced apples, sugar, flour, lemon juice and spices. Fill the pie shell with the mixture. Dot with butter. Cover with top crust, sealing edges well. Sprinkle with sugar and bake in a preheated 375 degree oven for approximately 50 minutes. Makes 8 servings.

PASTRY:

2	cups flour
1	teaspoon salt
2/3	cup shortening, very cold
1/4	cup very cold water

In large bowl, cut shortening into dry ingredients until mixture is crumbly. Using a fork, add the water in portions until ball is formed. Chill in refrigerator for 30 minutes. Divide in half. Roll each into a 15 inch circle, about 1/8 inch thick. In top crust, make several small slashes for venting.

MILLIONAIRE PIE

2	cups confectioners sugar
1/2	cup softened butter
1	large egg, beaten
1/4	teaspoon salt
1/2	teaspoon vanilla
2	cups Cool Whip
1	cup well drained, crushed pineapple
1/2	cup chopped nuts
2	baked 8 inch pie crusts

Cream together powdered sugar and butter. Add egg, salt and vanilla. Mix until light and fluffy. Spoon mixture evenly into pie crusts and chill. Mix together Cool Whip, pineapple and nuts. Spoon on top of egg mixture and chill. Keep refrigerated. Serves 6 per pie.

BREAD PUDDING

3	cups bread cubes
4	cups hot milk
1/2	cup sugar
3	eggs, beaten
4	tablespoons margarine, melted
1/2	teaspoon salt
1	teaspoon vanilla
3/4	cup raisins
1/4	teaspoon nutmeg
1/4	teaspoon cinnamon

Add bread cubes to hot milk; set aside to cool. Add remaining ingredients. Pour into buttered pan. Place pan with pudding into larger pan of hot water. Bake for 1 hour at 350 degrees. Serve warm with Whisky Hard Sauce.

WHISKY HARD SAUCE:

1-1/2	cup confectioners sugar
2	tablespoons butter, softened
1	tablespoon whisky

Stir together and let rest a few hours to blend flavors. If too thick, add a few drops of milk. Serve over bread pudding.

PECAN PIE

1	8 inch pastry shell
3	eggs
1/2	cup light corn syrup
1	cup sugar, white or brown
	dash of salt
1	teaspoon vanilla
1	cup chopped pecans
	pecan halves for garnish

Beat eggs until frothy. Add sugar, corn syrup, salt, vanilla and pecans. Mix well. Pour into pie shell. Arrange pecans on top. Bake in hot oven, 400 degrees, for 10 minutes. Lower temperature to 350 degrees and bake 30 minutes longer or until almost firm at center. Cool. Serves 6.

STRAWBERRY-RHUBARB PIE

1	pastry for Two Crust Pie
1 3/4	cups sugar
2/3	cup flour
1	teaspoon lemon juice
3	cups chopped rhubarb
	(about 3/4 inch dice)
3	cups sliced fresh strawberries
1	tablespoon butter or margarine

Heat oven to 400 degrees. Prepare pastry. Mix together the sugar, flour, and lemon juice. Stir in the strawberries and rhubarb. Pour into prepared pastry-lined pie pan. Dot with the butter or margarine. Cover

with the top pastry that has slits cut into it. Seal the edges and place a 2 inch wide strip of foil around the edge to prevent leaks and over browning. Bake about 55-60 minutes until browned and juice is bubbling through the slits. Remove foil and cool on a rack. Best if served slightly warm.

FUDGE BROWNIES

1	cup butter
4	squares chocolate
4	eggs
2	cups sugar
2	cups flour
1	cup nuts
2	teaspoons vanilla

Melt butter and chocolate together. Cool. Beat eggs and add the sugar. Combine the two mixtures and beat thoroughly. Add flour, nuts and vanilla. Spread into a shallow 8 inch square pan. Bake in preheated oven at 350 degrees for 25-30 minutes. Do not over bake. Cool and cut into squares. Yields 16 brownies.

APPLE CRISP

8- 9	tart apples, like Granny Smith
1 1/2	cups quick oats
1 1/2	cups brown sugar
1	cup flour
2	teaspoons cinnamon
1/4	teaspoon nutmeg
3/4	cup butter (1 1/2 sticks)

Arrange apple slices in a buttered deep baking dish. If apples are tart, add a sprinkling of granulated sugar over slices. Combine oats, sugar, flour and spices. Cut in butter. Mix well and spread over apples. Bake at 350 degrees for 35 to 40 minutes. Serve warm with cheese wedges or whipped cream. Serves 6 to 8.